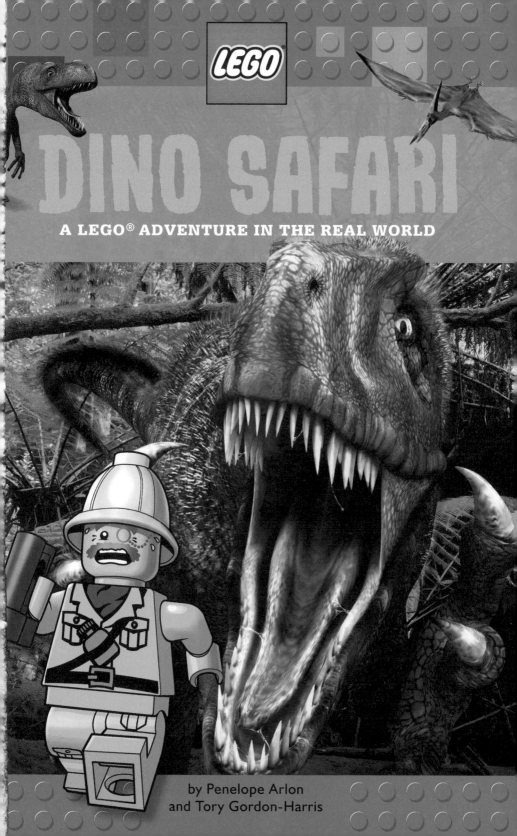

LEGO®

DINO SAFARI

A LEGO® ADVENTURE IN THE REAL WORLD

by Penelope Arlon
and Tory Gordon-Harris

Welcome, LEGO fans!

LEGO® Minifigures show you the world in a unique nonfiction program.

This leveled reader is part of a program of LEGO® nonfiction books, with something for all the family, at every age and stage. LEGO nonfiction books have amazing facts, beautiful real-world photos, and minifigures everywhere, leading the fun and discovery.

To find out about the books in the program, visit scholastic.com.

Leveled readers from Scholastic are designed to support your child's efforts to learn how to read at every age and stage.

LEVEL 1 READER
Beginning reader
Preschool–Grade 1
Sight words
Words to sound out
Simple sentences

LEVEL 2 READER
Developing reader
Grades 1–2
New vocabulary
Longer sentences

LEVEL 3 READER
Growing reader
Grades 1–3
Reading for inspiration
and information

Contents

BUILD IT!

Check out the epic building ideas when you see me!

Come on a dinosaur safari with us. Let's see how many dinosaurs we can spot!

I don't like the look of those raptors. I hope that there's nothing bigger out there . . .

Let's find dinos!

It's millions and millions of years ago. There are no houses, no cars, no phones. Our Earth is ruled by the biggest land animals ever—the dinosaurs. Dinosaur explorers need to watch their step.

Let's go! There were 700 kinds of dinosaurs. Let's find as many as we can!

I hear that I might be related to the dinos. I wonder if that's true!

The world is full of huge meat-eaters, and they are all hungry. Run! T. rex wants its breakfast!

BUILD IT!

Build a tall tower for the explorers to climb up and watch the dinosaurs from.

I'll keep you safe and show you what I know. Come on, dino spotters!

This probably isn't the best place for me . . .

◀ **Monolophosaurus**

Meat-eaters

Every day and night in dino world was a food fight. Dinosaurs were either looking for dinner or trying to not be dinner! Meat-eaters had terrible weapons. Huge, razor-sharp teeth crunched through bones like crackers. Claws tore through tough skin like paper. Smaller dinosaurs were just as deadly. They had speed and brains, too.

Some meat-munchers had teeth that curved backward to hold prey.

Utahraptor ➡

I think I can see the point of those . . . yikes!

ER60082

Giganotosaurus

Dilophosaurus

Argh! I'm glad that the dinos will be long gone before people arrive.

BUILD IT!

The explorers need somewhere to shelter. Quick, build a safe, dino-proof hideout!

Spinosaurus →

Arrgh! Spinosaurus is coming! Jump in the lake!

Think again! Spinosaurus could swim even faster than it could run!

Take a jaw full of terrifying teeth. Take claws that could slash through a bicycle. Add them to a huge, hungry dinosaur. Say hello to Spinosaurus.

HEARD THIS WORD?

predator: an animal that hunts and eats other animals

It's the biggest predator of all. Spinosaurus's jaws were as long as your mom or dad!

Compsognathus was built for speed. I'd better run and save my bacon!

← Compsognathus

A pack of hungry Velociraptors moves around a Protoceratops. The raptors can bring it down only if they work together. They have large claws on their feet, like daggers. Tiny, sharp teeth are ready to tear into Protoceratops's tough skin.

Protoceratops →

Racing raptors! They've formed a pack, but what are they hunting?

Oh, no! The raptors are after Hot Dog Man! Will they catch up?

Let's hope they don't like mustard.

Waaahh!

But Protoceratops fights back. It flicks its thick tail at the raptors. It bites with its sharp beak. Who will win?

Hmm . . . Protoceratops lived in a herd. But even with its friends, I don't think it could beat the raptors.

Velociraptor had a larger brain than other dinos. This was one smart dinosaur.

Velociraptor

Velociraptors could run at 40 miles per hour (64 kph) in short bursts.

Plant-eaters

Some dinosaurs ate only plants. You may think that these herbivores were a calm, friendly bunch. THINK AGAIN! They needed epic battle skills to fight off the meat-eaters. Some of them had horns for stabbing. Club-shaped tails could bash and slam. Thick skulls smashed against one another. Thumb spikes gave nasty pokes.

Look at the large, bony bumps. That sharp beak gives me goose bumps, though!

Ankylosaurus

Pachycephalosaurus

← Torosaurus

← Iguanodon

HEARD THIS WORD?

herbivore: an animal that eats only plants

Skin a quarter inch (6 mm) thick! My suit of armor is no match for that.

What's the best way to keep safe from a meat-eater? Have thousands of friends to protect you! Many plant-eaters lived in herds, or groups. There could be 10,000 dinosaurs in just one herd. If a dinosaur had no friends—it had to RUN! Gallimimus was one of the fastest. It could run as fast as a racehorse.

- What's worse than one croc coming for dinner?
- Two crocs coming for dinner!

← Edmontosaurus

Okay, let's see how fast this dino can go. They say that it ran at 40 miles per hour (64 kph)!

Gallimimus →

Dino fight! It's meat-eater against plant-eater. Allosaurus wants a meal. But it's not going to be easy. Stegosaurus has plates on its back. That's not the place to attack. Allosaurus lunges at the neck. In a flash, Stegosaurus swipes its deadly tail at the meat-eater. But Allosaurus is smart and fast. It will figure out how to get its huge jaws around the plant-eater. Who will win?

Allosaurus's short arms didn't help this meat-eater. It needed big, strong arms that punch like mine . . .

Allosaurus

If Allosaurus won, it had enough food to eat for two weeks.

This is making me hungry. How about enough pizza for two weeks? Yum!

← **Stegosaurus**

The best way to not be eaten was to be ENORMOUS. Plant-eaters needed to be REALLY enormous, because meat-eaters were supersized, too. How big was Argentinosaurus? This plant-eater was so big that you couldn't get your arms around its leg! Look up at a three-story building. That's how tall this dinosaur was!

Argentinosaurus ➡

At nearly 100 tons, this dino was about as heavy as a jet.

Imagine all the trees that it trampled and mammals that it squished. Let's fly out of here!

BUILD IT!

Think big, and build the most gigantic dinosaur you can imagine.

This vast dino was nearly as long as two tennis courts. That's aces!

19

Dig up a dino

When people first dug up dinosaur bones, they thought that the bones were from giants or dragons. It's not hard to see why! Some are gigantic. Dinosaur bones were buried over time. After millions of years, some of them turned into rocks, called fossils. Paleontologists dig up fossils and fit them together like jigsaw puzzles. They sometimes get it wrong!

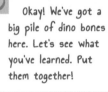

Okay! We've got a big pile of dino bones here. Let's see what you've learned. Put them together!

Hmm . . . just put them together, she says. Where does this one go?

I think you need to bone up on your dinosaurs . . .

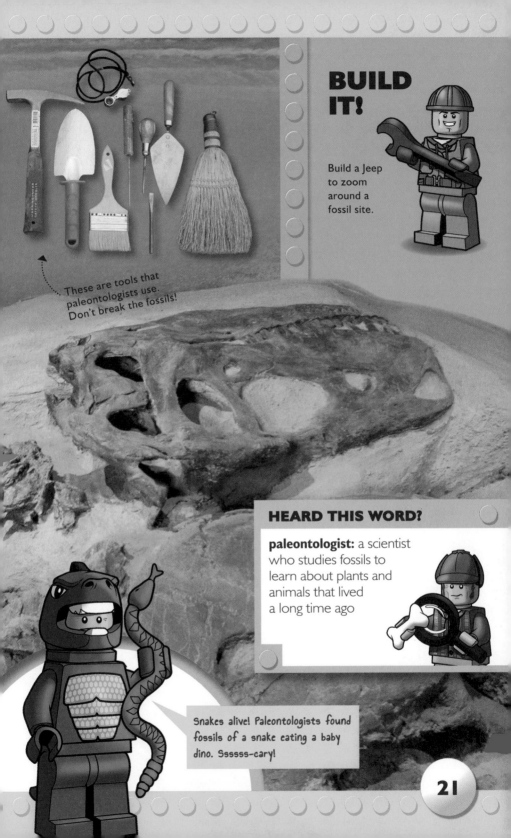

BUILD IT!

Build a Jeep to zoom around a fossil site.

These are tools that paleontologists use. Don't break the fossils!

HEARD THIS WORD?

paleontologist: a scientist who studies fossils to learn about plants and animals that lived a long time ago

Snakes alive! Paleontologists found fossils of a snake eating a baby dino. Sssssss-cary!

Ever seen dino poop? It's not just bone fossils that tell us about dinosaurs. There are other clues, too. Footprints in rock show how big a dinosaur was. The distance between footprints can often tell us how fast the dino ran. Dino egg fossils have also been found. Giant poop fossils can tell us what dinos ate!

Stand back! I need to make sure that this dino poop has lost its stink!

This Therizinosaurus egg is the biggest dino egg ever!

There is a bone in this dino's poop, showing its last lunch.

Hmm . . . what can I tell about this dinosaur from the shape of its skull?

Aha! I've discovered a dinosaur nest. Look at all these eggs!

That's no nest. It's a T. rex toilet. And you're hugging a load of old poop!

23

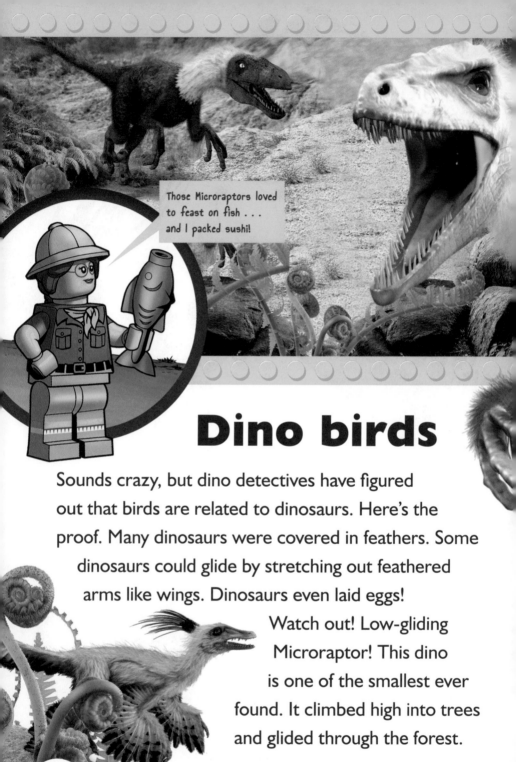

Those Microraptors loved to feast on fish . . . and I packed sushi!

Dino birds

Sounds crazy, but dino detectives have figured out that birds are related to dinosaurs. Here's the proof. Many dinosaurs were covered in feathers. Some dinosaurs could glide by stretching out feathered arms like wings. Dinosaurs even laid eggs!

Watch out! Low-gliding Microraptor! This dino is one of the smallest ever found. It climbed high into trees and glided through the forest.

Deinonychus ➤

Nobody knows what color the feathers were. They may have been pink!

Are you seriously telling me that I am related to those dinos?

Absolutely, birdbrain!

A group of Maiasaura moms has found a perfect place to lay eggs. It's a hungry world out there! The dinos nest close to one another for safety. They scoop out shallow holes. Each mother lays 30 to 40 eggs in her nest. Then mom and dad cover

Some dino eggs were the size of chicken eggs. Others were as big as footballs! Ouch!

This nest is egg-cellent . . . Aaarrrrgh!

the nest with rotting plants to keep the eggs warm. When the babies hatch, they are small and weak. The mother has to look after them.

BUILD IT!

How would you keep baby dinos safe? Build a nest with your bricks.

I wonder what noises these dinosaurs made. Did they sing like birds?

A newborn dino hatchling was about the same length as your school ruler.

Good-bye, dinos!

About 65 million years ago, something terrible happened. The big dinosaurs suddenly disappeared. It seems likely that a huge meteorite fell from space. It hit Earth with a massive BANG! It caused earthquakes all over the world. Dust clouds may have blocked sunlight. Many plants died out. There was nothing for the dinosaurs to eat.

HEARD THIS WORD?

meteorite: a piece of rock or metal from space that lands on Earth

Not even I can put this one out. Call 911!

BUILD IT!

It's the end of the dinosaurs! Build a meteorite to crash into your dino world.

Quick! Let's go, before we blow! It looks like the end of our dino safari. But is it really all over?

Don't worry. Remember, birds are related to dinosaurs!

Hmm . . . I'm suddenly feeling a bit spooked by all these birds . . .

Build a LEGO® dino world!

It's a minifigure adventure in dinosaur world! Use your stickers to fill the desert landscape. Look out for the Velociraptors! There may be others hiding nearby . . .

Amazing dino words

detective
A person who solves mysteries.

earthquake
A sudden, violent shaking of the Earth.

fossil
A bone, shell, footprint, or other trace of an animal or plant from millions of years ago, preserved as rock.

glide
To move through the air smoothly and easily.

hatchling
A baby animal that came out of an egg.

herbivore
An animal that eats only plants.

herd
A group of animals that live or travel together.

meteorite
A piece of rock or metal from space that lands on Earth.

paleontologist
A scientist who studies fossils to learn about plants and animals that lived a long time ago.

predator
An animal that hunts and eats other animals.

prey
An animal that is hunted and eaten by another animal.

safari
A trip to see wild animals in their natural surroundings.

skull
The set of bones in the head that protects the brain.

Dino names

Allosaurus
AL-uh-SOR-uhs

Ankylosaurus
ANG-kuh-luh-SOR-uhs

Argentinosaurus
AHR-juhn-TEE-nuh-SOR-uhs

Compsognathus
kahmp-SAHG-nuh-thuhs

Deinonychus
dye-nah-NIK-uhs

Dilophosaurus
dye-LOH-fuh-SOR-uhs

Edmontosaurus
ed-MAHN-tuh-SOR-uhs

Gallimimus
gal-uh-MYE-muhs

Giganotosaurus
JEE-gan-oh-tuh-SOR-uhs

Iguanodon
ig-WAH-nuh-dahn

Maiasaura
MYE-uh-SOR-uh

Microraptor
MYE-kroh-RAP-tur

Monolophosaurus
MAHN-uh-loh-fuh-SOR-uhs

Pachycephalosaurus
pak-ee-SEF-uh-luh-SOR-uhs

Protoceratops
proh-toh-SER-uh-tahps

Spinosaurus
SPYE-noh-SOR-uhs

Stegosaurus
STEG-uh-SOR-uhs

Therizinosaurus
THER-uh-ZEE-nuh-SOR-uhs

Torosaurus
TOR-oh-SOR-uhs

T. rex
TEE reks

Utahraptor
YOO-tah-RAP-tur

Velociraptor
vuh-LAH-suh-RAP-tur

I'm going to get my buns out of here before those dinos see me!

31

LEGO

DEEP DIVE

A LEGO® ADVENTURE IN THE REAL WORLD

by Penelope Arlon
and Tory Gordon-Harris

Welcome, LEGO fans!

LEGO® Minifigures show you the world in a unique nonfiction program.

This leveled reader is part of a program of LEGO® nonfiction books, with something for all the family, at every age and stage. LEGO nonfiction books have amazing facts, beautiful real-world photos, and minifigures everywhere, leading the fun and discovery.

To find out about the books in the program, visit scholastic.com.

Leveled readers from Scholastic are designed to support your child's efforts to learn how to read at every age and stage.

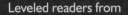

LEVEL 1 READER

Beginning reader
Preschool–Grade 1
Sight words
Words to sound out
Simple sentences

LEVEL 2 READER

Developing reader
Grades 1–2
New vocabulary
Longer sentences

LEVEL 3 READER

Growing reader
Grades 1–3
Reading for inspiration
and information

Contents

BUILD IT!

Check out the epic building ideas when you see me!

Come on an incredible undersea adventure. There's so much to see in the sea.

I might just explore from inside this sub. It looks a bit fishy out there.

Dive deep!

We have better maps of the surface of Mars than of our ocean. Dive in! There is so much to explore. Almost three-quarters of our Earth is covered in ocean. Some parts are 7 miles (11 km) deep. The ocean is filled with amazing creatures.

Let's go! There are more than a million plants and animals in the ocean. I want to see a shark!

I'm after a shipwreck and a ton of treasure!

Hope you spot some amazing fish. Catch you later!

But watch out, divers. Some are dangerous. Look out! Shark fin! This is going to be a wild adventure!

BUILD IT!

Build the best-ever submarine to explore the ocean.

Hey, King! Make me a huge wave to carry me through the book!

Don't find yourself in deep water!

Let's hope that these divers don't get into any hot water. I'll be watching.

Coral reef

Did you know? A third of all fish live in coral reefs.

Can you see that flash of pink? Only a few yards below the waves is a world of color. Coral reefs are the largest living things on our planet. They look like rock, but they are made up of tiny sea creatures. Coral is alive! Coral reefs are home to more

HEARD THIS WORD?

shoal: a large group of fish

Whoa! Have you lost your brain?

No, silly! That brain-shaped rock is actually coral!

sea life than anywhere else in the ocean. That flash of pink is a shoal of fish. Find a purple-spotted sea slug. Watch a turtle swim by with flapping fins.

BUILD IT!

The divers really need an underwater exploration station. Fill it up with cool tools for exploring.

- What is the strongest creature in the sea?
- A mussel!

39

It's eat or be eaten on the reef. Dull colors help animals hide. Bright colors can show that a creature is poisonous. The colors yell, "Don't eat me!" Animals also take care in other ways. The puffer fish can blow itself up to twice its original size.

Down here, there are a few rules. You can look at the animals, but remember the rule about no touching. Got it?

Look at that awesome octopus. Ahh, it wants a huge, eight-armed hug!

Watch out! Some octopus bites can kill in minutes! That octopus is armed, fully armed!

The most important thing to remember in the sea is DON'T TOUCH ANYTHING.

Are sea animals more colorful than land animals?

Puffer fish blow up and pop out their spines.

The blue-ringed octopus is one of the most poisonous animals in the whole ocean.

This is creepy. I feel like I'm being followed . . .

- What did the seaweed say when it was stuck to the bottom of the sea?
- Kelp, kelp!

E-04

Swim away from the reef into an underwater forest. Keep still, and the forest comes to life. Giant seaweeds, called kelp, grow on the seafloor. They grow all the way up to the water's surface. Splash! A seal dives down to search for a tasty meal. The fish swim into the shady weeds to hide. The spiky sea urchins keep safe. They are too prickly to eat!

BUILD IT!

Build an underwater forest for your divers to hide in.

This is one strange forest. Kelp can grow to 150 feet (46 m). I'm glad that I don't have to chop this down!

Sailfish sometimes leap out of the water. Woo-hoo, we're both catching waves!

Open ocean

Far from the beach, there are thousands of miles of open ocean. Fish swim in huge shoals. Sailfish are the fastest predators in the ocean. A team of sailfish swims around a shoal of sardines. The sardines swim into a tight ball. They swim close to keep safe.

But the sailfish are not the kings of the ocean. The great white shark shoots upward. Its massive mouth is open wide. The sailfish flee. The shark can smell blood from 3 miles (5 km) away. It speeds toward its prey at 15 miles per hour (24 kph). One bite of its 300 teeth, and the sardines are lunch.

I can understand crossing an ocean for a good hot dog, but for jellyfish? Really?

Some sea creatures travel halfway across the open ocean to find food. One turtle was tagged and tracked. She laid her eggs on a beach in Indonesia. Then she swam all the way to the coast of Oregon, in the United States. She traveled 12,774 miles (20,558 km). She crossed the whole Pacific Ocean to find jellyfish—her favorite snack!

BUILD IT!

Build a turtle strong enough to swim across the ocean.

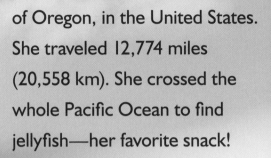

beach
2 mi. (3 km)

jellies
12,772 mi. (20,555 km)

I've been following this reptile for days. I'm seasick of this now. Are we there yet?

Sigh . . . another 10,000 miles (16,090 km) to go. I'll be on this ship for over a year!

Leatherback turtles flap their flippers like birds flap their wings, to "fly" through the water.

Check out these ocean giants. The whale shark is the biggest fish in the world. It's as long as a bus. But it doesn't eat anything larger than your littlest fingernail! A lion's mane jellyfish has tentacles that are longer than a blue whale. Imagine seeing a shoal of manta rays as big as small planes flapping past.

The whale shark swims with its mouth open, scooping up tiny plants and animals to eat. Jaw-dropping!

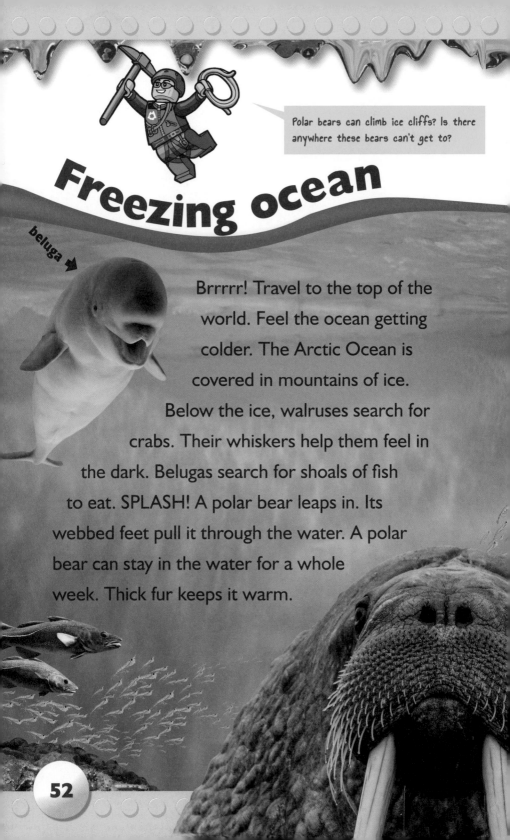

Polar bears can climb ice cliffs? Is there anywhere these bears can't get to?

Freezing ocean

beluga →

Brrrrr! Travel to the top of the world. Feel the ocean getting colder. The Arctic Ocean is covered in mountains of ice. Below the ice, walruses search for crabs. Their whiskers help them feel in the dark. Belugas search for shoals of fish to eat. SPLASH! A polar bear leaps in. Its webbed feet pull it through the water. A polar bear can stay in the water for a whole week. Thick fur keeps it warm.

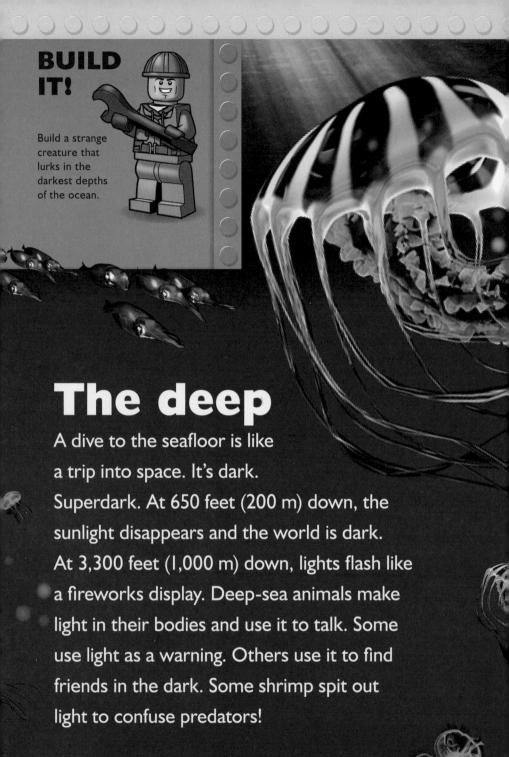

BUILD IT!

Build a strange creature that lurks in the darkest depths of the ocean.

The deep

A dive to the seafloor is like a trip into space. It's dark. Superdark. At 650 feet (200 m) down, the sunlight disappears and the world is dark. At 3,300 feet (1,000 m) down, lights flash like a fireworks display. Deep-sea animals make light in their bodies and use it to talk. Some use light as a warning. Others use it to find friends in the dark. Some shrimp spit out light to confuse predators!

Humans know more about the surface of the Moon than the bottom of the ocean.

Arrgh! It's a glow-in-the-dark shark! The lantern shark lights up to warn predators to keep away.

Are you kidding me? There are sharks down here, too? Lights off, buddy. We're trying to explore.

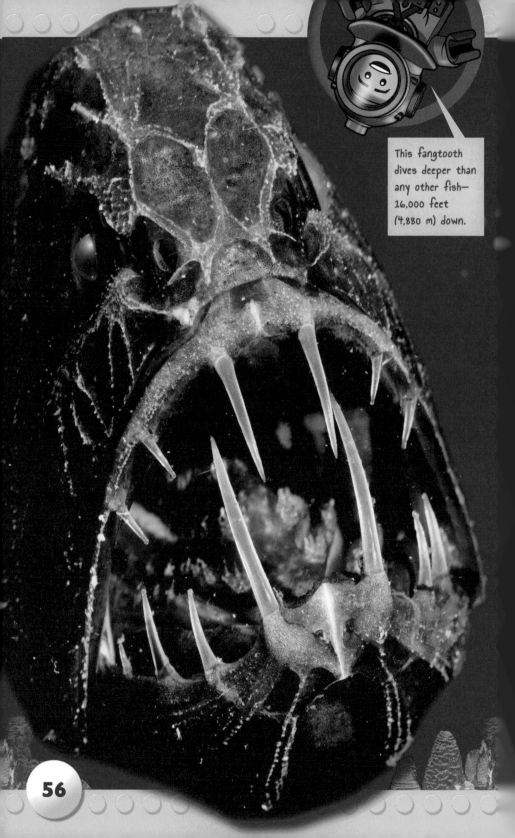

This fangtooth dives deeper than any other fish— 16,000 feet (4,880 m) down.

The creatures of the deep are very strange. It's like they just swam out of a scary movie! Hairy crabs and huge clams live by underwater chimneys that spit out hot liquid. The fangtooth can't shut its mouth like we can—its teeth are too long! The dumbo octopus is as big as a beach ball. Those things sticking out of its head are fins, not ears. It's out of this world down in the deep.

dumbo octopus →

Careful, dude, that sizzling-hot seawater can get up to 700°F (370°C).

We don't want to get into hot water. Let's go.

Shipwreck!

HEARD THIS WORD?

shipwreck: the remains of a ship that has sunk or been destroyed at sea

Before there were airplanes, more things were taken across the ocean by ship. But there were dangers at sea. Greedy pirates searched the seas, stealing ships and their treasures.

Whoa! Some of the wrecks down here are hundreds of years old!

That doesn't mean that I'm not still around to protect my treasure!

Fa la la. In the past, sailors believed that if they heard a mermaid's song, the ship would sink. Oops!

Every so often, ships were wrecked on rocks or icebergs. Others were destroyed by storms or fire. There may be as many as 3 million shipwrecks lying on the ocean floor.

BUILD IT!

Build a ship, but make it look as if it has been sitting at the bottom of the ocean for 100 years!

Shiver me timbers! There's a shipwreck! Let's find the treasure. Unless someone else has gotten there first. Ships that sank took their treasures with them. Find a sunken pirate ship, and it may be filled with stolen jewels, gold, and coins. There are hundreds of wrecks still to be found. It's the world's biggest treasure hunt!

If you find a wreck, and there isn't an owner looking for it, you can keep the loot. This treasure is mine!

I saw it first. Let's share it!

Build a LEGO® reef!

It's a minifigure adventure in the ocean! Fill the coral reef with your colorful stickers. Who is the shark sneaking up on? Make sure that your divers can escape from any danger!

Amazing ocean words

armor
A metal covering worn to protect the body in battle.

bill
An animal's hard, pointy jaws.

dinosaur
A reptile, often very large, with four legs and scaly or feathered skin. Dinosaurs died out 65 million years ago.

jellyfish
A sea creature with a soft, see-through body and long tentacles.

kelp
A large brown plant that grows in the sea.

mussel
A sea animal that lives in a long black shell.

pirate
A person who attacks and steals ships at sea.

poisonous
Capable of causing sickness or death.

predator
An animal that hunts and eats other animals.

prey
An animal that is hunted and eaten by another animal.

reptile
An animal with scaly skin that lays eggs. Turtles are reptiles.

shipwreck
The remains of a ship that has sunk or been destroyed at sea.

shoal
A large group of fish.

shrimp
A small sea animal with a shell and a long tail.

tentacle
An animal's long, thin body part, used for movement and for feeling and holding things. Jellyfish have tentacles.

Help! I'm done down here. Get me back to dry land before I see that pesky shark again . . .

BUG OFF!

A LEGO® ADVENTURE IN THE REAL WORLD

by Penelope Arlon
and Tory Gordon-Harris

Welcome, LEGO fans!

LEGO® minifigures show you the world in a unique nonfiction program.

This leveled reader is part of a program of LEGO® nonfiction books, with something for all the family, at every age and stage.

LEGO nonfiction books have amazing facts, beautiful real-world photos, and minifigures everywhere, leading the fun and discovery.

To find out about the books in the program, visit scholastic.com.

What's bugging you?

Leveled readers from Scholastic are designed to support your child's efforts to learn how to read at every age and stage.

LEVEL 1 READER

Beginning reader
Preschool–Grade 1
Sight words
Words to sound out
Simple sentences

LEVEL 2 READER

Developing reader
Grades 1–2
New vocabulary
Longer sentences

LEVEL 3 READER

Growing reader
Grades 1–3
Reading for inspiration
and information

Contents

BUILD IT!

Check out the epic building ideas when you see me!

I've heard there are up to 10 million kinds of insects. I've only spotted one!

Buggy world

Bugs are mini, but mighty. They have been on Earth for nearly 500 million years and live on every continent.

Let's explore the world of bugs! From mini mites to mega beetles, insects come in all sizes.

I'm headed for the rain forest. That's where the most types of bugs live.

There are about 200 million bugs for every person on the planet.

BUILD IT!

Build a superbug. Make sure it has lots of legs and huge wings!

There are lots of types of bug that have never been spotted before . . . by anyone!

I want to find bugs that can fly loop-the-loop and even fly backward! Tally ho!

Who's who?

We use the word "bug" to talk about tiny creatures that live on land. Bugs can be divided into groups. You can often tell which group a bug belongs to by counting its legs. But be quick! Some bugs are fast!

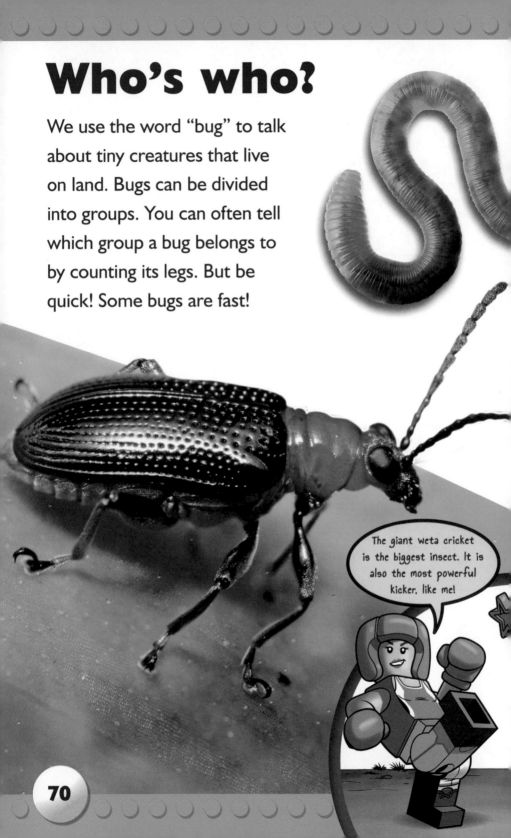

The giant weta cricket is the biggest insect. It is also the most powerful kicker, like me!

Segmented worm: no legs

Mollusk, like slugs and snails: no legs

HEARD THIS WORD?

antennae: feelers on some bugs' heads that look like little sticks.

Insect, like ladybugs and ants: 6 legs

Arachnid, like spiders and scorpions: 8 legs

Woodlouse: 14 legs

The tiniest insect is the fairyfly. It's smaller than the dot over this letter i. Sweet!

Centipede and millipede: lots and lots of legs

71

Some bugs behave badly. They bite! They sting! They carry germs! But most bugs are good guys. They stop our world from being super smelly. Every day, animals drop lots of poop. The dung beetle makes poop into a ball. It then rolls the ball away to eat or lay its eggs in.

Millions of insects eat up dead leaves and wood on the forest floor. Their poop makes the soil rich for growing plants.

BUILD IT!

Build a big garbage truck that can help recycle, just like the bugs do!

73

Why do bees have sticky hair? Because they have honeycombs!

Want an apple for lunch? Thank a bug! Bugs carry pollen from one flower to another. This means that plants can make seeds and fruit. Honey bees sip sweet nectar from flowers. They will use it to make honey. As they sip, pollen sticks to them. They carry the pollen to another flower, where there's more nectar to sip!

pollen: the yellow plant dust that is carried to other plants so that they can produce seeds.

Thank you, bees, for all this yummy honey. It takes thousands of bees to make just one pot of honey!

That's a lot of work! I guess that's where the saying "busy as a bee" comes from! Yikes! I don't think they want to share.

Incredible insects

All insects have three body parts—a head; a thorax
with the legs attached; and an abdomen, which
is usually the biggest part. They also have
three pairs of jointed legs, antennae,
and some have wings. Insects
have all sorts of amazing
abilities. Fireflies can
light up their bodies.
Fleas can jump
150 times their
own height!

Pond skaters
don't need a boat. They
can walk right across water.
Their light bodies barely
dent the surface.

2509

Insects come in a rainbow of colors. Sometimes their colors say, "I taste gross." Other times they warn, "STAY AWAY!" The brightest bugs are the most dangerous. They are usually poisonous to their predators.

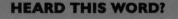

HEARD THIS WORD?

predator: an animal that hunts and eats other animals.

Ancient Egyptians made colorful jewels in the shape of beetles.

I can top that! The ancient Mayans wore LIVE beetles as jewelry.

BUILD IT!

Design and build an insect that is so colorful, it will never be eaten!

79

Some insects have another way of avoiding predators. They look exactly like the nature around them. They can't be eaten if their enemy can't spot them. They might mimic a stick, or a leaf. Can you spot the insects in these pictures?

This caterpillar looks just like bird poop. No one will want a bite of it!

. . . eight, nine, ten. Coming, ready or not!

Tee hee! Fly Monster will NEVER spot me in these flowers.

Oops, you left your antennae sticking up. Found you!

The most incredible insects of all live in the forests of North and South America. Thousands of leafcutter ants work together.

They cut and carry small pieces of leaves across the forest floor. Each piece can be 50 times as heavy as the ant carrying it. The ants live in underground nests, where they eat fungus that grows on the chewed leaves.

I spy with my mini eye . . . some helpful insects in the garden.

Insects help plants grow and they nibble pests. Take a hike, pests!

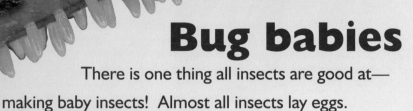

Bug babies

There is one thing all insects are good at—making baby insects! Almost all insects lay eggs. They lay them somewhere safe, like under a leaf or in wood. Most insect parents leave their eggs alone and the babies take care of themselves.

Termite queens can lay 30,000 eggs in one day. Imagine that!

That's ten million eggs a year! I've got my hands full with one baby!

Insects often lay their eggs on a leaf so it can be their babies' first meal.

Shield bugs are a bit different. The female lays eggs and then guards them until the nymphs (babies) hatch.

BUILD IT!

Build a submarine so your bug explorers can search for mosquito eggs in the water!

85

Eggs

Larva

Pupa

Do you love butterflies?
They start life looking very
different. Butterfly eggs hatch
into caterpillars. A caterpillar
eats and eats and eats. It grows
up to 100 times bigger. Then
it becomes a pupa.

Beetles, flies, bees,
and ants go through
three stages before they
turn into adults.

HEARD THIS WORD?

pupa: the stage between larva and adult. Some insects build a shell around themselves.

Butterfly

After weeks or months, the pupa breaks open and a butterfly flies out!

Creeping and crawling

Do you find bugs gross? Or creepy? The bugs that seem the most creepy are often the most incredible. Slugs and snails are bug super movers. They leave a trail of slimy mucus which helps them move smoothly, even upside down. They are super strong. Snails can carry up to ten times their own weight!

Did you know slugs have more teeth than sharks? They've got up to 27,000 chompers to rip food into bits.

Snail slime is incredible stuff. Scientists think it can heal our skin.

Let's fix you up, Clumsy Guy. It's slime time for you!

89

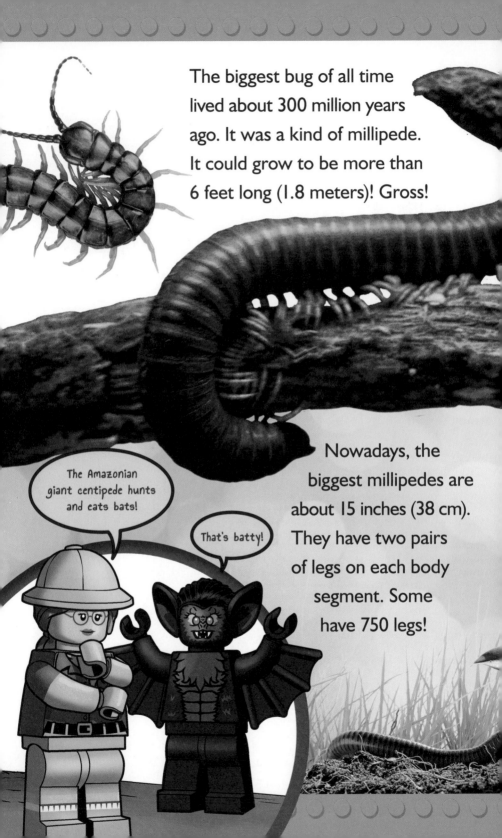

The biggest bug of all time lived about 300 million years ago. It was a kind of millipede. It could grow to be more than 6 feet long (1.8 meters)! Gross!

Nowadays, the biggest millipedes are about 15 inches (38 cm). They have two pairs of legs on each body segment. Some have 750 legs!

The Amazonian giant centipede hunts and eats bats!

That's batty!

BUILD IT!

Build a centipede. How many legs does it have?

Centipedes have one pair of legs on each body segment. They also have a pair of fangs to help them hunt other bugs.

If a group of millipedes formed a soccer team, they would need more than 4,000 pairs of cleats!

Octan

In the web

Spiders give some people the creeps.
But they are probably the coolest bugs
around. All spiders spin silk. Some weave
them into beautiful webs. Webs are made
to catch insects. Silk is also used to wrap up
eggs to keep them safe. One spider even
makes a little net that it drops on
insects to catch them!

A spider's web
is one of the
strongest materials
on the planet.

Whoa! Where did all these spiders come from?

Relax, my pet spider's eggs have hatched. She laid over 1,000 eggs and there are more to come!

orb weaver

tarantula

It's bugtastic!

It's a minifigure adventure in bug world!
Use your stickers to decorate the
undergrowth. Put some bugs in
the sky, too!

I hope you've had fun learning all about amazing bugs. But me? I've got to fly!

Amazing bug words

arachnid
A bug with eight legs and two body sections. Spiders and scorpions are arachnids.

fungus
A living thing that is neither a plant nor an animal. A mushroom is a fungus.

insect
A land bug that has three body sections and six legs.

larva
An insect after it hatches from its egg, but before it becomes an adult. Two or more larva are called larvae.

nectar
A sweet liquid made by plants, especially by flowers. It is used by bees to make honey.

segment
Parts of an animal that when put together make the whole animal. A worm has segments.

silk
A thin thread that is made in some bugs' bodies, such as spiders.

web
The net a spider spins with silk in order to catch insects.

LEGO®

MIGHTY MACHINES

A LEGO® ADVENTURE IN THE REAL WORLD

RD 04

Welcome, LEGO fans!

LEGO® minifigures show you the world in a unique nonfiction program.

This leveled reader is part of a program of LEGO® nonfiction books, with something for all the family, at every age and stage. LEGO nonfiction books have amazing facts, beautiful real-world photos, and minifigures everywhere, leading the fun and discovery.

To find out more about the books in the program, visit scholastic.com.

Leveled readers from Scholastic are designed to support your child's efforts to learn how to read at every age and stage.

LEVEL 1 READER	LEVEL 2 READER	LEVEL 3 READER
Beginning reader	Developing reader	Growing reader
Preschool–Grade 1	Grades 1–2	Grades 1–3
Sight words	New vocabulary	Reading for
Words to sound out	Longer sentences	inspiration and
Simple sentences		information

BUILD IT!
Check out the epic building ideas when you see me.

If you see a word in **bold**, you can find out what it means on page 127.

Hey, can I have a lift? I need to get to the end of this book!

Look around you. Machines help out everywhere! Giant diggers lift tons of dirt. Long trains pull cars full of people. Rockets blast into space.

Start your engines. Let's go!

BUILD IT!
Build your own mighty machine. Will it have wheels or wings?

Make way! Longest road train coming through!

Let's build a road! Call in the digger. The digger has an arm called a boom. It has a bucket on the end. The sharp teeth **scoop** out dirt.

The biggest digger in the world could hold 4,000 soccer balls.

Awesome! I'll kick them in. GOAL!

The biggest diggers are as heavy as 400 cars!

BUILD IT!
Build a digger. How many LEGO bricks can you scoop up?

The biggest dump truck tire is as tall as 100 minifigures!

The dump truck brings dirt and rocks to make the road. It may hold about 25 tons of dirt.

That's as heavy as 5 big elephants! It tips out the dirt ready for the bulldozers.

Call in the bulldozer! The bulldozer uses a big **blade** to push the dirt and rocks. It makes everything flat. A super dozer has a blade that is as wide as 462 minifigures!

Our road needs
to go through
that old building.

Stand back! I'm
going to blow
the building up.

Oops. Wrong one!
Quick, where's
the bulldozer?

The bulldozer has
giant tracks to help
it move. I'd better
make tracks!

Bring in the steamroller!
It may weigh 20 tons.
It smoothes **asphalt**
onto the road.
Now the road is built.
Let's drive!

Help! I don't want to become a flatbread!

Chill out, man. It's only traveling at 2 miles per hour!

BUILD IT!

Build cars, motorcyles, and trucks for your road. Create a huge traffic jam!

Concrete is good for building. The concrete mixer has a barrel that turns round and round. It mixes cement, rock, and water to make concrete. When the concrete is poured out, it hardens.

Ooh, I'm sinking into this concrete.

Careful! Concrete turns hard really quickly.

Yikes! I'm not going to stick around to find out!

How do you build a super-
tall building? A crane can lift
what you need! The tallest
crane can lift things up to
70 **stories** high.

BUILD IT!

Build a crane with a super-long arm. Remember to build a strong base for it!

I said pick up the bar, not my car!

Some machines are used
to carry things. Honk honk!
The road train is on its way.
It can pull up to 100 **trailers**!
Road trains are the longest
trucks in the world.

Oh no, I think we've got a puncture.

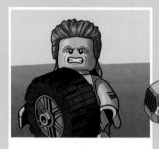

Are you kidding me? There are 100s of tires to check.

Found it, finally! Yawn. That's tired me out . . .

BUILD IT!

Build a road train. How many trailers will it have?

Some trucks can carry other heavy things. A car transporter carries between 5 and 10 cars. The cars drive on and off **ramps**.

BUILD IT!
Build a car transporter to carry cars all around your house.

Heeeeave!

Cars weigh about 2 tons each! That's heavy.

All aboard! The **cargo** ship travels all over the world. It holds more than 2,000 big boxes. One ship may be as long as 13 blue whales!

Check this out! The biggest cargo ship can hold more than 745 million bananas!

Toot Toot! Trains pull cars full of people.

Can you tell me where the bathroom is please?

I'm afraid it's at the other end of the train.

Argh! This train is over half a mile long!

The longest trains have 44 cars.
One train in Japan travels at
375 mph!

Tickets, please!
Hurry up, this train
is super-speedy!

Zoom! The Airbus jet flies at 540 mph. It holds more than 500 people.

The Airbus can fly 8 miles up in the air! Give me a window seat!

It is the biggest plane in the world. It has two levels!

BUILD IT!
Build an awesome plane and take your minifigures on vacation.

AIRBUS A380-800

3, 2, 1, blast off! The Soyuz rocket blasts into space. It moves at 755 feet per second. It takes astronauts to a **space station**.

Look, aliens! But how did they get there?

We've got company. Let's get the flying saucer.

Hello there! Anyone up for a space race?

It's the mightiest machine of all!

BUILD IT!
Build a rocket to carry LEGO bricks into space. Perfect for building your space station!

125

Build a LEGO® construction site!

Mighty machines love to work. What will you build today?

Mighty machine words

asphalt
a black material that is used for making roads.

blade
the broad, flat part of a machine that pushes the material to be moved.

cargo
something that is carried from one place to another by a vehicle.

concrete
a hard, strong material that is used for building.

ramp
a slope that joins two surfaces of different heights.

scoop
to dig out.

space station
a large spacecraft in which people live, to do research and experiments.

story
a part of a building where all the rooms are on the same level—also called a "floor."

trailer
A wagon that carries heavy loads and is pulled by another vehicle.

This ax is no good. Bring in the mighty machines!

It's good to learn some mighty words!

EMERGENCY!

A LEGO® ADVENTURE IN THE REAL WORLD

Welcome, LEGO fans!

LEGO® minifigures show you the world in a unique nonfiction program.

This leveled reader is part of a program of LEGO® nonfiction books, with something for all the family, at every age and stage. LEGO nonfiction books have amazing facts, beautiful real-world photos, and minifigures everywhere, leading the fun and discovery.

To find out about the books in the program, visit scholastic.com.

Leveled readers from Scholastic are designed to support your child's efforts to learn how to read at every age and stage.

LEVEL 1 READER

Beginning reader
Preschool–Grade 1
Sight words
Words to sound out
Simple sentences

LEVEL 2 READER

Developing reader
Grades 1–2
New vocabulary
Longer sentences

LEVEL 3 READER

Growing reader
Grades 1–3
Reading for inspiration and information

Contents

BUILD IT!

Check out the epic building ideas when you see me!

Got an emergency? We're on it.

Find out about the hometown heroes who help in this book. Let's go!

Emergency!

Help! Emergency! Call 911 and an emergency team will leap into action. Off they go! They zoom to the rescue, no matter where you are. On land, in the air, even at sea, they are ready to help. Find out about some awesome heroes and the amazing jobs they do every day. Let's go!

Firefighters are always ready to help. They work as a team. One hero is great, but a whole team of them is AWESOME!

The coolest part of a rescue team? The vehicles! Find out about them inside.

BUILD IT!

Build an emergency vehicle. How fast will it speed to the rescue?

The police make sure everyone follows the rules. Make sure YOU don't speed through this book!

I'm awesome, but the everyday heroes who help are the REAL superstars.

Fire!

Make way! Lights flashing and sirens screaming, the fire truck speeds to the rescue. Fires can spread fast, so fire trucks need to get there quickly. The firefighters use long hoses to spray water on the flames. Nozzles at the end of the hose help control the jets of water.

Big fires need plenty of water to put them out. Special tanker fire trucks can carry over 1000 gallons (3,785 liters) of water. That's enough water to fill 47 bathtubs. This fire will be out in no time!

Oh no! The hoses can't reach this fire. No problem—call in the ladder truck! Some fire trucks carry giant ladders to reach tall buildings. The firefighter climbs onto a platform, then WHOOSH! The ladder stretches up toward the building. The ladder may reach as high as 100 feet (30.5 m). That's as high as 762 minifigures standing on top of each other.

Firefighters usually work a 24-hour shift. They cook, sleep, and do chores at the station.

When an emergency call comes in, they take action, even if it is dinnertime!

Help! That poor guy's cape is on fire. Call the fire department immediately!

Stop! It's just my fiery fashion sense. Now my cape is all wet!

BUILD IT!

Build a very tall building. Then build a very long ladder that can reach the top!

DETROIT FIRE DEPARTMENT

41 DETROIT

526

Help! A wildfire is burning out of control! Wildfires are super dangerous. They can spread at nearly 15 miles per hour (24 km/h), destroying everything in their path. This is no job for a regular fire engine. Bring on the fire plane and its brave pilots! The largest planes can dump 12,000 gallons (54,553 liters) of water onto the flames.

So firefighters protect my beautiful forest from the air AND on the ground?

Yep. We clear trees and brush from the area ahead of the fire to "starve" it. Hard work takes teamwork!

HEARD THIS WORD?

wildfire: A large and dangerous fire that burns out of control in a forest or grassland area.

Call the police!

Uh-oh, someone has broken the law. The police zoom to the scene of the crime with loud sirens and flashing lights. In an emergency, the police can drive very fast. Police cars can speed at 155 miles per hour (249 km/h)— twice as fast as a cheetah!

The police have plenty of jobs to do. They catch criminals, find lost or stolen things, and keep people safe. The police use all kinds of vehicles for their work. Motorcycles and cars get them to an emergency fast. But if the police need to keep an eye on a large area, they use a helicopter. Helicopters can hover in the sky like an insect, while the police look around.

Hey you, let me in! It's the police. There's been a robbery at the local gym.

Aha! It looks like I've caught you red-handed. What do you have to say for yourself?

Um, these are just my boxing gloves. They're only good for stealing last-minute knockouts . . .

Ocean heroes

The police aren't the only heroes making a splash on the ocean. If someone gets lost at sea, the coast guard is off to the rescue. Their boats and helicopters use special equipment called radar.

The coast guard carries out more than 100 rescue missions a day.

Can I be a coast guard, too? I'm a great swimmer and an expert in merm-aid.

Radar uses radio
waves to find lost
things, even deep
in the ocean.

Ahoy, me hearties!
My pirate ship is in
a spot of trouble.
I need a rescue!

Your ship isn't the ONLY
thing in trouble. Is that a
STOLEN treasure chest I
can see?

This old chest? That's
just where I keep my
spare peg leg!

Hospital heroes

When someone is sick or injured, they need treatment fast. Woo woo woo! An ambulance races to the scene within minutes. It's like a hospital on wheels! And the paramedics at the wheel know just what to do.

The paramedics work fast. They help out at the scene and then take people to a hospital if they need more care.

BUILD IT!

Build an ambulance able to dodge through traffic at top speeds. Don't forget to add flashing lights!

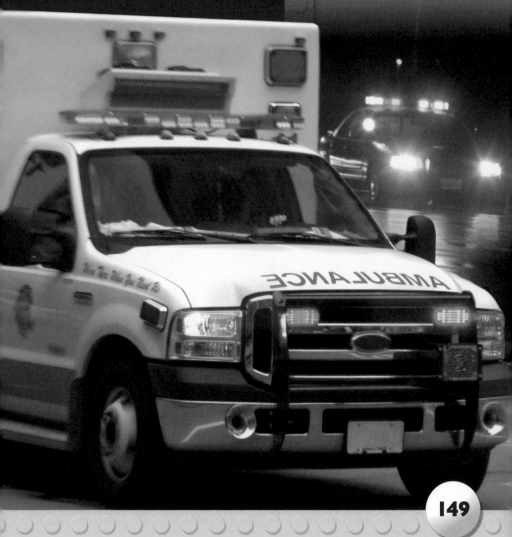

Ambulances can travel at more than 100 miles per hour (160 km/h), but sometimes that isn't fast enough. Vroom, Vroom! Paramedics on special motorcyles can travel at up to 141 miles per hour (255 km/h). They can squeeze in and out of traffic.

I can do awesome tricks on my mighty machine, but these motorcycle heroes can save lives.

You again? It's the third time this week? What's happened now?

Well, there was this guy eating a banana and, well, you can guess the rest of the story . . .

They can reach places that other ambulances can't. They carry enough equipment to save lives.

Oh no! Someone is injured. A regular ambulance would take hours to reach them. Who can help? Look up in the sky. It's an air ambulance. This helicopter can land in a space as small as a tennis court. In Australia, the Royal Flying Doctor Service uses air ambulances every day. They can reach patients who live hundreds of miles into the countryside.

Who needs my help? I've just landed in the front yard, and the hospital has a team waiting.

Excuse me, this is an AIR ambulance, not a BEAR ambulance! Sigh, I'll do my best to help.

Mountain rescue

Look at that view! But the weather changes quickly in the mountains. Steep paths twist and turn. Someone is lost. It's hard for a rescue team to find them. They need tough vehicles with big tires to grip the rocky ground.

It takes awesome pilot skills to move through the mountains. I'm on it!

A helicopter can help. It hovers in the air. Its crew lowers a rope to rescue people from tight spots. Good work, rescue team!

Rescue

It's freezing today in the mountains. Snow is piled high. A skier is stranded! A snowmobile has skis of its own so it can glide over the snow. It has tracks at the back to grip the icy ground. Woof woof! The rescue dog will help, too. He is trained to sniff out people who are lost in the snow.

Good dog! The snowmobile has lifesaving equipment on board. Its driver can also speed hurt people off the mountain to get help.

Just dropping in to find out what you've learned.

BUILD IT!

Create a super-speedy snowmobile to race over the highest snowdrifts.

To the rescue!

It's another busy day for the minifigure emergency services. Use your stickers to show them rushing to the rescue. Don't forget helicopters flying high in the sky!

LICE LINE • DO NOT CROSS • POLICE LINE

Emergency words

Criminal
Somebody who
breaks the law.

Emergency
A serious problem
that needs to be
fixed right away.

Hover
To stay in one place
in the air.

(The) Law
A long list of rules that
everybody in a country
has to follow. Stealing
is against the law.

Nozzle
A round part at the end
of a hose that is used to
control how fast the
water sprays out.

Paramedic
A person who drives
an ambulance or
motorcycle and who
knows emergency
treatment but is
not a doctor.

Patient
A person who needs
help from a doctor,
nurse, or paramedic.

Patrol
To travel around an
area and check what
is happening there.

Radar
A machine that can
find boats and other
objects in the sea or
the sky. Airplanes
also have radar.

Stolen
Something that
has been taken
from someone
without asking.

Did you read this
book cover to cover?
You see, I'm an
undercover cop.

DO NOT CROSS

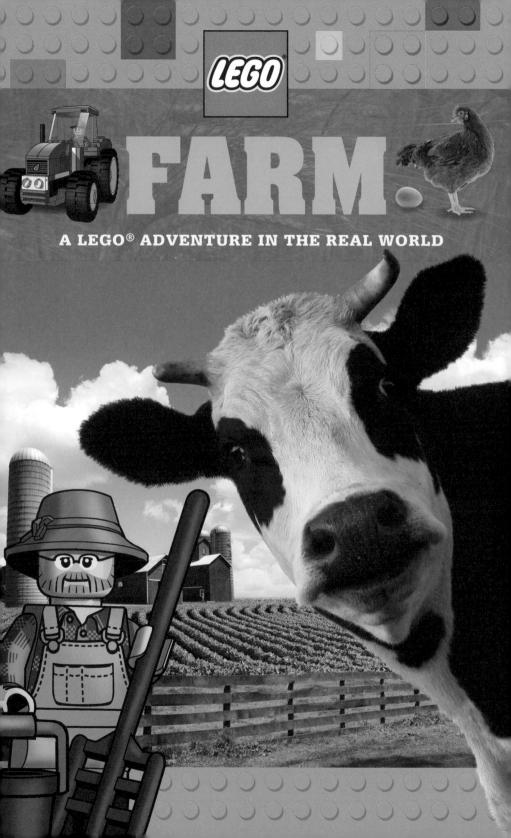

LEGO® minifigures show you the world in a unique nonfiction program.

This leveled reader is part of a program of LEGO® nonfiction books, with something for all the family, at every age and stage. LEGO nonfiction books have amazing facts, beautiful real-world photos, and minifigures everywhere, leading the fun and discovery.

To find out more about the books in the program, visit scholastic.com.

Leveled readers from Scholastic are designed to support your child's efforts to learn how to read at every age and stage.

LEVEL 1 READER

Beginning reader
Preschool–Grade 1
Sight words
Words to sound out
Simple sentences

LEVEL 2 READER

Developing reader
Grades 1–2
New vocabulary
Longer sentences

LEVEL 3 READER

Growing reader
Grades 1–3
Reading for inspiration and information

BUILD IT!

Check out the epic building ideas when you see me.

Hey! Can I have a ride? I need to get to the end of this book!

It's morning on the farm.
What's happening today?
Let's hop on the tractor and
explore. Who's in the barn?

Most of the food you eat comes from farms. You're welcome!

I wanted to be a farmer, but it was too eggs-hausting!

Farms are busy places, with animals to feed and crops to grow.

BUILD IT!
Create your own farm. You'll need a house to live in and a barn for your animals to sleep in.

There are 2.2 million farms in the US.

My favorite farms are ones that grow carrots!

Cluck, cluck! Let's go to the chicken coop. The chicken has laid an egg! She lays four or five eggs a week— that's about 200 per year.

She's a busy bird!

Oink, oink! These little piglets are hungry! The mommy pig, or sow, feeds milk to her piglets. Pigs are really smart. They talk to each other using grunts and squeals.

Keep it down! Pigs can squeal nearly as loud as a jet!

Phew, it's hot today! I need to cool down.

Here! I'll help you. Pigs keep cool by rolling in mud.

Well, I'm cool, but now I need a shower . . .

One cow can produce over 80 glasses of milk a day! That's a-moo-zing!

BUILD IT!
Build a huge tanker truck to keep the milk cool and take it to supermarkets.

The biggest milkshake ever was made in a tanker truck. It made 50,000 drinks!

Big animal farms are called ranches. This one has more than 1,000 cows. Cowboys and cowgirls use horses to round them up.

Cows are fast moo-vers. They can run at 25 miles per hour (40 km/h).

I hope they don't get lost. This ranch is bigger than 1,000 soccer fields!

Cowboys and cowgirls use lassos to catch cows.

Yee-haw! Watch this. Bull's-eye!

Yikes! I think I need a bit more practice . . .

Watch the cute baby lambs leaping and bouncing in the field. Lambs can walk when they are a few minutes old.

Lambs know their mom's call in a field full of noisy sheep.

You're not my mommy!

They have thick woolly fleeces to keep them warm.

BUILD IT!
Build a barn for your sheep to sleep in when it's cold. Make it warm and cozy!

The lambs are all grown up and their fleeces are long and shaggy. Phew! It's too hot. It's time for a haircut.

Pweeeeee! I use whistles to tell my sheepdog what to do. Stop! You're a sheepdog, not a bird dog!

A sheepdog herds the sheep together. The farmer cuts the fleece. The fleece is then turned into wool.

The wool from one sheep can make eight sweaters or 50 pairs of socks.

Can you knit? My sweater and socks have holes in them.

Only a tractor can drive across bumpy, muddy fields. Huge wheels with knobby tires help grip the ground. Hold on tight, it's a bumpy ride!

Most tractors travel at around 25 miles per hour (40 km/h). Slow, but steady!

Woohoo! This car is FAST! Race you across the field!

This is the easiest race I've ever won!

Uh-oh, I guess I'm stuck in second place.

The biggest tractor tire is 58 LEGO minifigures high!

Tractors aren't fast, but they pull all kinds of useful farm machines. Plows make the soil ready for crops.

Plow

Sprayer

Baler

Trailer

Sprayers water crops. Balers collect crops in neat bundles.

BUILD IT!
Build a tractor and a farm machine for it to pull. Don't get stuck in the mud!

Oink, oink!

My tractor is strong enough to pull this trailer, even when it's full of heavy pigs!

Most of the plants you eat, such as wheat, rice, fruit, and vegetables grow on farms. These plants are called crops.

Corn is tasty! It's also used in cooking oil, paint, and soap!

Did you know that corn is actually a type of grass?

183

It's harvest time! Grain crops, such as wheat, need to be cut when they're ripe. A combine harvester cuts the crops and then removes the seeds (grain), the part we eat.

Later, this grain will be ground into flour for bread and cakes. I wish my combine harvester could bake cakes, too!

7636

5000

Combine harvesters cut at 7 miles per hour (11 km/h), but they do lots of jobs at once!

BUILD IT!
Design a farm vehicle. What can it do? How does it help the farmer?

Cozy! I'd love a nap!

The leftover stalks are useful, too. They're turned into straw for pets' beds.

185

Most fruit grows
best in hot countries.
These oranges are
ripe and ready
to be picked.

There are
over 7,000 different
types of apple.
Yummy!

Bananas grow in bunches. Guess how big the biggest one was.

OK, one banana, two bananas, three . . .

It was 473 bananas! I'll show you . . .

Bananas are the number one fruit crop in the world—100 billion of them are eaten every year. How many do you eat?

Farmers don't just grow things for us to eat. Cotton farms grow cotton to make fabric, oil, and animal feed.

Read all about it! Tree farms are the best because they give us wood and paper.

I like flower power. Flower farms are so colorful.

A one-acre (4,047 m²) cotton field can help make 325 pairs of jeans!

BUILD IT!
Design and build your own farm. What will you grow on your farm?

Vroom! The rubber for my tires comes from rubber tree farms.

Farms are awesome! Many crops are used to make medicines.

Farm words

barn
a farm building for animals to sleep in or used to store grain and machines

coop
a shelter where chickens can lay their eggs

crop
a plant that is grown on farms

dairy farm
a farm where cows are milked

fleece
a sheep's woolly covering

grain
seeds taken from plants that can be eaten

harvest
when ripe crops are cut and collected

ranch
a large farm, usually for animals, such as cows

ripe
ready to be harvested or eaten

sow
a female pig

stalk
the long, straight part of a crop that other smaller parts grow out of

tractor
a farm vehicle that can pull other machines, such as trailers

I love farms, but I'm a little scared of cows . . .

Don't be such a chicken!